Math Counts

Shape

Introduction

In keeping with the major goals of the National Council of Teachers of Mathematics Curriculum and Evaluation Standards, children will become mathematical problem solvers, learn to communicate mathematically, and learn to reason mathematically by using the series Math Counts.

Pattern, Shape, and *Size* may be investigated first—in any sequence.

Sorting, Counting, and *Numbers* may be used next, followed by *Time, Length, Weight,* and *Capacity.*

Ramona G. Choos, Professor of Mathematics, Senior Adviser to the Dean of Continuing Education, Chicago State University; Sponsor for Chicago Elementary Teachers' Mathematics Club

About this Book

Mathematics is a part of a child's world. It is not only interpreting numbers or mastering tricks of addition or multiplication. Mathematics is about *ideas.* These ideas have been developed to explain particular qualities such as size, weight, and height, as well as relationships and comparisons. Yet all too often the important part that an understanding of mathematics will play in a child's development is forgotten or ignored.

Most adults can solve simple mathematical tasks without the need for counters, beads, or fingers. Young children find such abstractions almost impossible to master. They need to see, talk, touch, and experiment.

The photographs and text in these books have been chosen to encourage talk about topics that are essentially mathematical. By talking, the young reader can explore some of the central concepts that support mathematics. It is on an understanding of these concepts that a child's future mastery of mathematics will be built.

Henry Pluckrose

1995 Childrens Press® Edition
© 1994 Watts Books, London, New York, Sydney
All rights reserved.
Printed in the United States of America.
Published simultaneously in Canada.
1 2 3 4 5 6 7 8 9 0 R 04 03 02 01 00 99 98 97 96 95

Math Counts

Shape

By Henry Pluckrose

Mathematics Consultant: Ramona G. Choos,
Professor of Mathematics

CHILDRENS PRESS®
CHICAGO

Look at the shape of this page.
Run your fingers
around the edges of the page.
What shape did you trace?

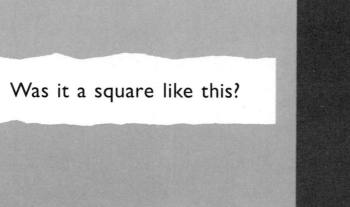

Was it a square like this?

Was it a circle like this?

5

Was it a hexagon like this?

Was it a rectangle
like this?

Was it a triangle
like this?

Squares, circles, triangles, rectangles,
and hexagons are regular shapes.
Each shape is easy to recognize.
What shape can you see here?

In what ways are these squares
similar to each other?
In what ways are they different?

In what ways are these triangles similar to each other?
In what ways are they different?

9

We can find regular shapes almost anywhere—squares,

circles,

rectangles,

triangles,

13

and even
hexagons.

14

We also can find regular shapes
in the world of nature.
This is a honeycomb made by bees.
Each honeycomb cell has 6 sides.
Each side is the same length.
Each cell is a hexagon.

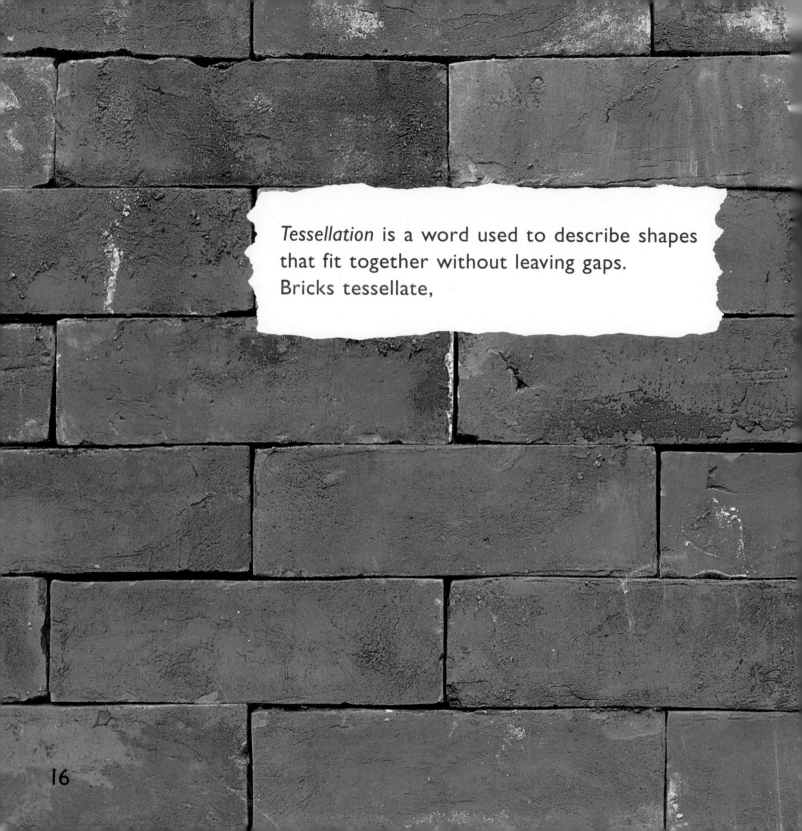

Tessellation is a word used to describe shapes that fit together without leaving gaps. Bricks tessellate,

16

and so do wooden blocks like these.

17

You can put some shapes
so close together that they touch.
Do circles tessellate?

Will these triangles
fit together
so that no spaces
are left between them?

Sometimes the shape of things seems to change when we look at them from a different angle. What shape are these cans?

These are
the same cans.
Now they seem
to be a different shape.

21

What shapes can you recognize here?

What shapes can you see now?

23

Shapes are everywhere.
Some are used to give messages
to drivers.
What do these signs mean?

What shapes can you find
in each of them?
Why are some road signs
set in a circle?
Why are others in a triangle?

25

Many things are shaped for their job.
Why is a clock face round?

QUARTZ

Why aren't wheels square?

27

Look for shapes
inside other shapes.
How many regular shapes
can you find in this bicycle

and in this steam engine?

30072

Not everything has a regular shape.
Clouds have ever-changing shapes
and so do trees as they sway in the wind.

You have a shape too,
but it is not made up
of squares and circles.
How is your face different
from the face of this clown?

31

Library of Congress Cataloging-in-Publication Data

Pluckrose, Henry Arthur.
   shape / Henry Pluckrose.
     p.   cm.
   Originally published: London; New York: F. Watts, 1988.
   (Math counts)
   Includes index.
   Summary: Photographs of familiar objects introduce basic shapes of squares, circles,
rectangles and triangles.
   ISBN 0-516-05456-2
   1. Geometry — Juvenile literature. [1. Shape 2. Geometry.] I. Title.
QA445.5.P547 1995
516'.15 — dc20   94-36350
                                                                              CIP
                                                                              AC

Photographic credits: Chris Fairclough, 4, 5, 6, 7, 8, 9, 10, 11, 12, 13, 14, 16, 17, 18, 19, 20, 21,
22, 23, 26, 27, 28, 30; Eye Ubiquitous © Roger Chester, 15; Unicorn Stock Photos, top right and
bottom left © Aneal Vohra, bottom right © Robert W. Ginn, 24; © Aneal Vohra (3 photos), 25;
© J. Winkle, 29; ZEFA, 31

Editor: Ruth Thomson
Assistant Editor: Annabel Martin
Design: Chloë Cheesman

INDEX